spot

PETS

DOGS

by Mari Schuh

AMICUS | AMICUS INK

ears

leash

Look for these words and pictures as you read.

tail

dog bowl

Woof! Woof!
Max barks loudly.
He sees a squirrel.

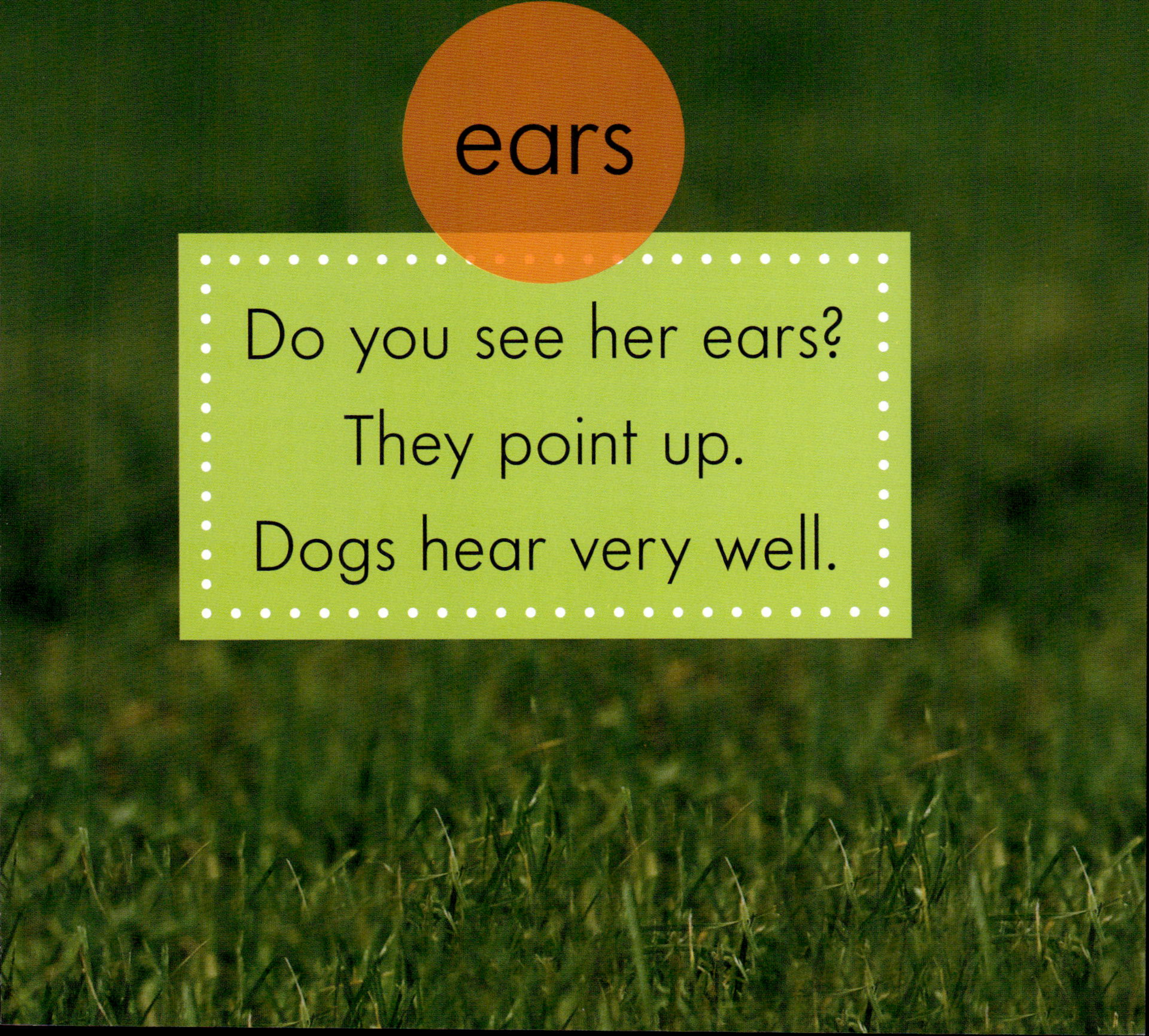

ears

Do you see her ears?
They point up.
Dogs hear very well.

leash

Do you see the leash?

It's time for a walk!

Dogs need to exercise every day.

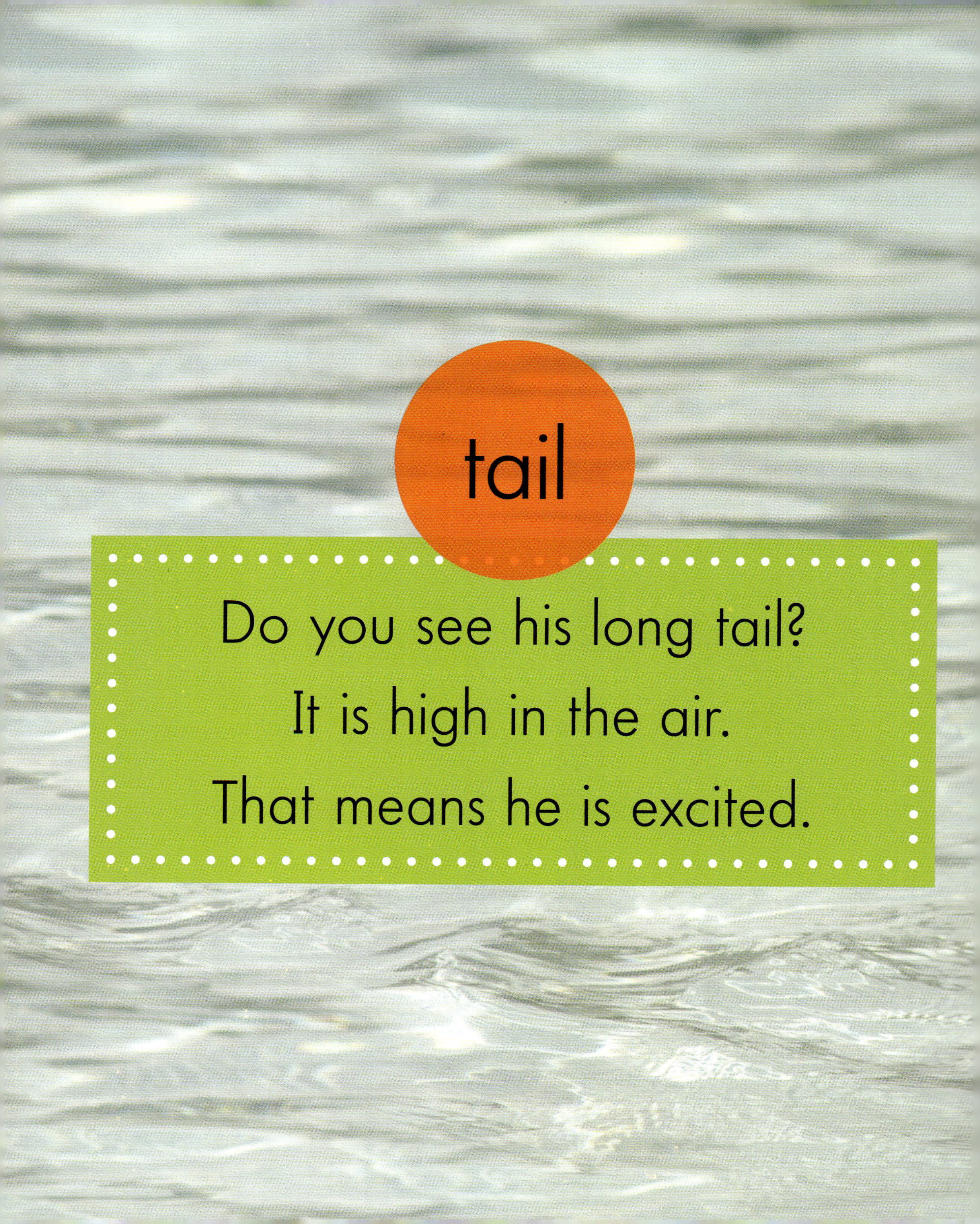

tail

Do you see his long tail?
It is high in the air.
That means he is excited.

Do you see the dog bowl?
Koji eats canned dog food.
His owner feeds him
two times a day.

dog bowl

Dogs are smart.
They can learn tricks.

Bella learns a new trick.
She rolls over.
Good dog!

ears

leash

Did you find?

tail

dog bowl

Spot is published by Amicus and Amicus Ink
P.O. Box 1329, Mankato, MN 56002
www.amicuspublishing.us

Library of Congress Cataloging-in-Publication Data
Names: Schuh, Mari C., 1975- author.
Title: Dogs / by Mari Schuh.
Description: Mankato, Minnesota : Amicus/Amicus Ink, [2019] | Series: Spot. Pets | Audience: K to grade 3.
Identifiers: LCCN 2017035726 (print) | LCCN 2017041653 (ebook) | ISBN 9781681514482 (pdf) | ISBN 9781681513669 (library bound) | ISBN 9781681522869 (pbk.)
Subjects: LCSH: Dogs--Juvenile literature.
Classification: LCC SF426.5 (ebook) | LCC SF426.5 .S3397 2019 (print) | DDC 636.7--dc23
LC record available at https://lccn.loc.gov/2017035726

Printed in China

HC 10 9 8 7 6 5 4 3 2 1
PB 10 9 8 7 6 5 4 3 2 1

In memory of Thunder —MS

Wendy Dieker, editor
Deb Miner, series designer
Ciara Beitlich, book designer
Holly Young, photo researcher

All photos courtesy of iStock except Dreamstime 10-11; Shutterstock cover, 4-5, 6-7